Seasons On Lookout Mountain II

Michèle Vachon Beaudin

Mentone, Alabama USA

(c)2012 immi'ges & words press
All rights reserved

Prints can be purchased separately by contacting
us for pricing and details.

Book And Cover Design by Michèle Vachon Beaudin

www.immiges.com
www.immigesandwords.com

michele@immiges.com

ISBN 978-0-9826877-2-7

Library of Congress Control Number: 2012949500

Printed in the United States of America

First Edition

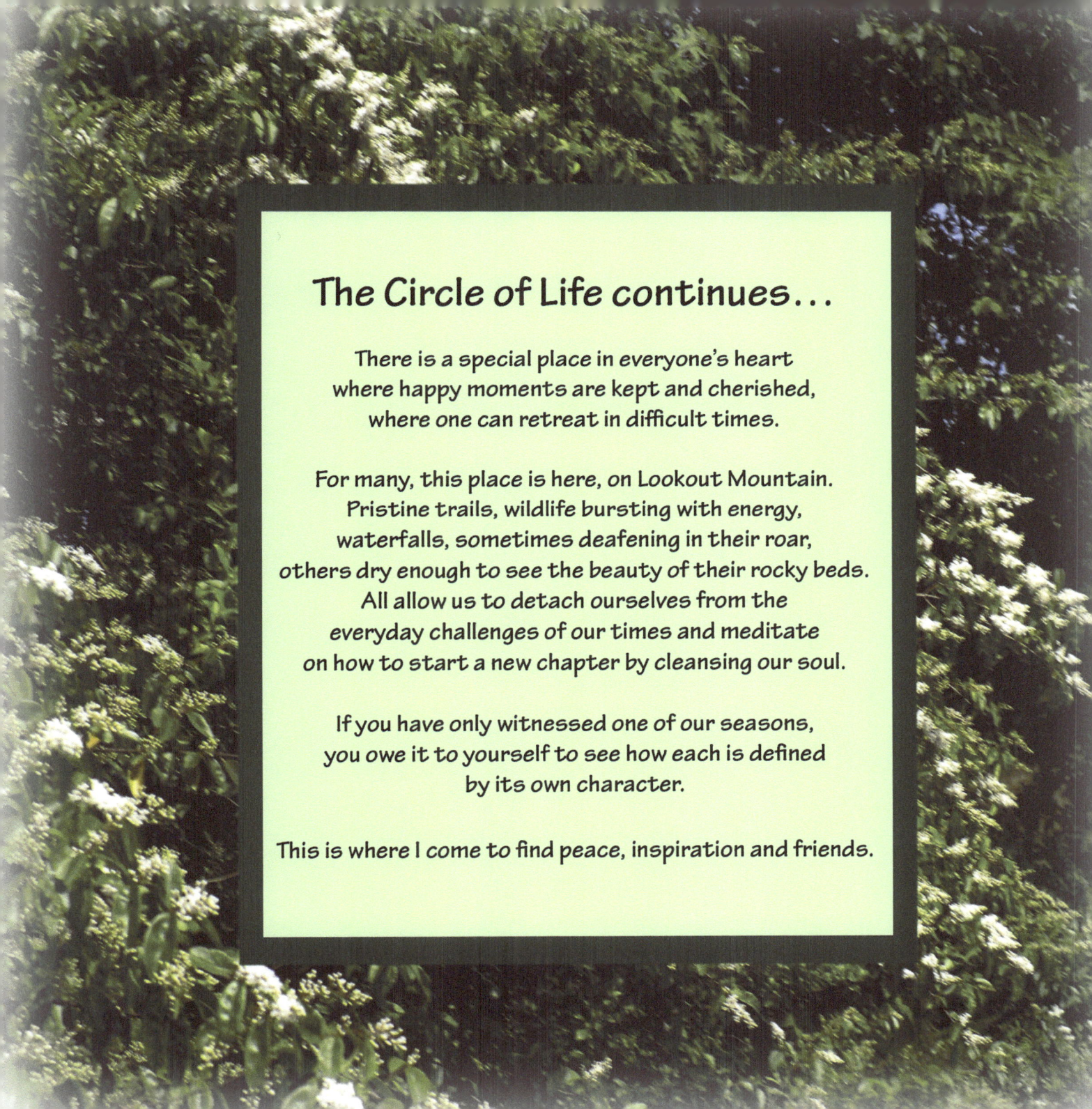

The Circle of Life continues...

There is a special place in everyone's heart
where happy moments are kept and cherished,
where one can retreat in difficult times.

For many, this place is here, on Lookout Mountain.
Pristine trails, wildlife bursting with energy,
waterfalls, sometimes deafening in their roar,
others dry enough to see the beauty of their rocky beds.
All allow us to detach ourselves from the
everyday challenges of our times and meditate
on how to start a new chapter by cleansing our soul.

If you have only witnessed one of our seasons,
you owe it to yourself to see how each is defined
by its own character.

This is where I come to find peace, inspiration and friends.

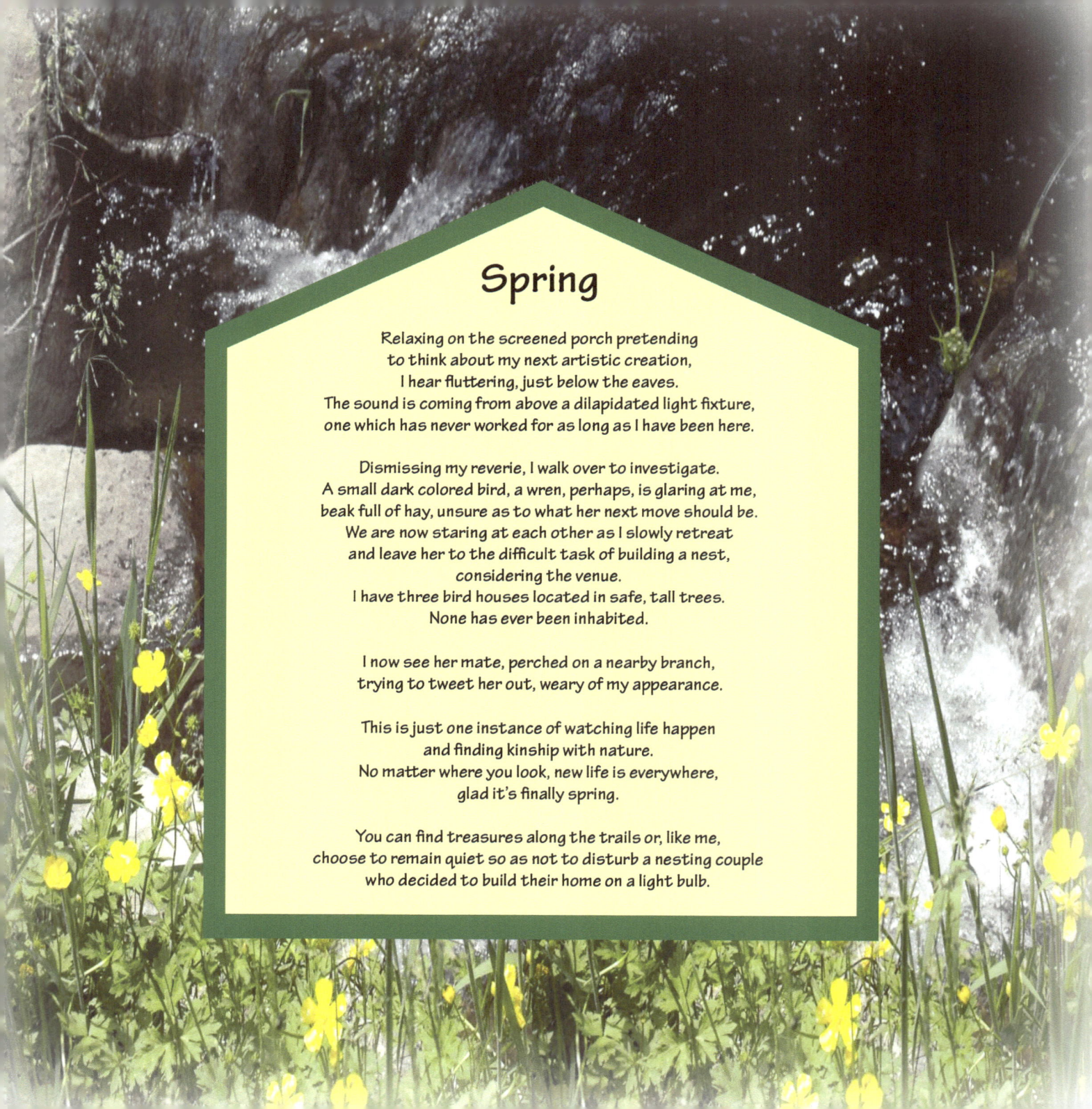

Spring

Relaxing on the screened porch pretending
to think about my next artistic creation,
I hear fluttering, just below the eaves.
The sound is coming from above a dilapidated light fixture,
one which has never worked for as long as I have been here.

Dismissing my reverie, I walk over to investigate.
A small dark colored bird, a wren, perhaps, is glaring at me,
beak full of hay, unsure as to what her next move should be.
We are now staring at each other as I slowly retreat
and leave her to the difficult task of building a nest,
considering the venue.
I have three bird houses located in safe, tall trees.
None has ever been inhabited.

I now see her mate, perched on a nearby branch,
trying to tweet her out, weary of my appearance.

This is just one instance of watching life happen
and finding kinship with nature.
No matter where you look, new life is everywhere,
glad it's finally spring.

You can find treasures along the trails or, like me,
choose to remain quiet so as not to disturb a nesting couple
who decided to build their home on a light bulb.

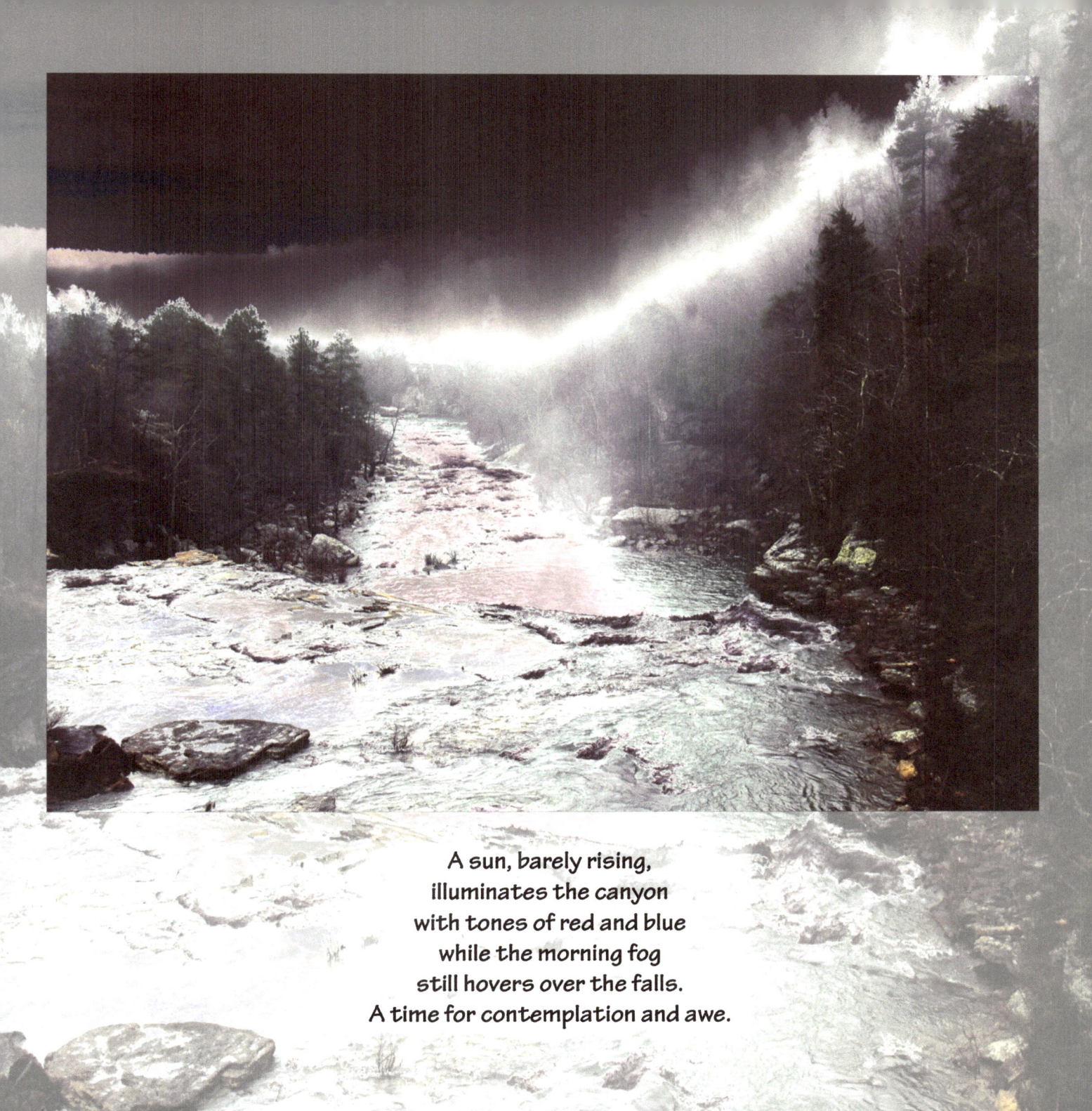

A sun, barely rising,
illuminates the canyon
with tones of red and blue
while the morning fog
still hovers over the falls.
A time for contemplation and awe.

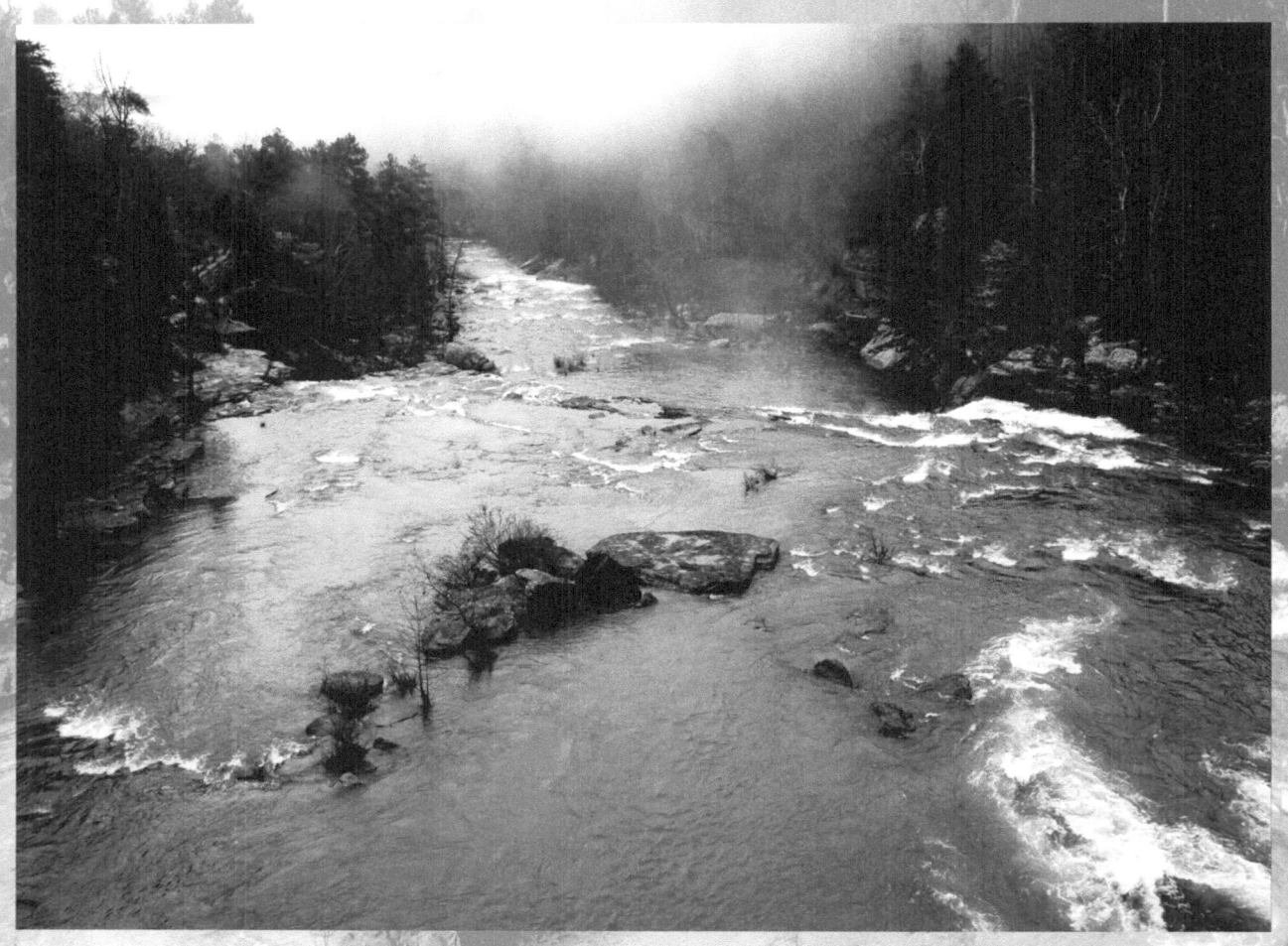

Time passes and light finally penetrates this world.
The trees adopt new shapes and
the scene takes on tinges of brown and green.
Night creatures have crawled back into their lairs,
as crows start exchanging words
above the roaring falls.

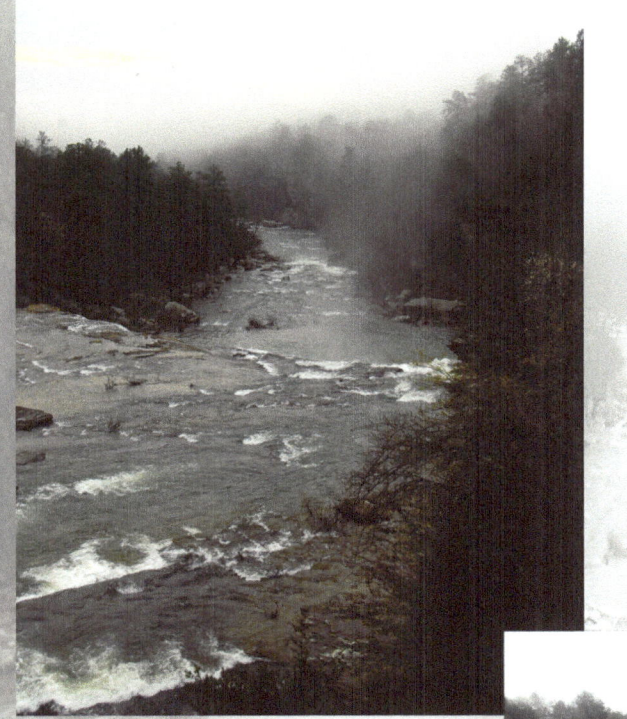

Morning is here.
Early spring blooms,
hidden behind the dark night,
are coming back
to life on the Little River bank.

Time for all to awaken
and bask in the glory
of a world that never
ceases to amaze.

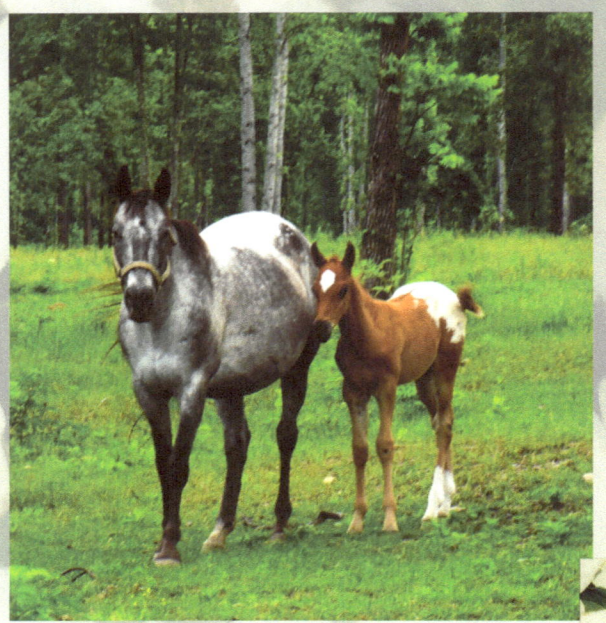

Flowers now abound,
summer
is around the corner.
Mothers tend to
their newborn.

A warm day
brings back
joyful sounds from
new life on the farm.
All can freely roam
in the pasture.

And...
love goes on.

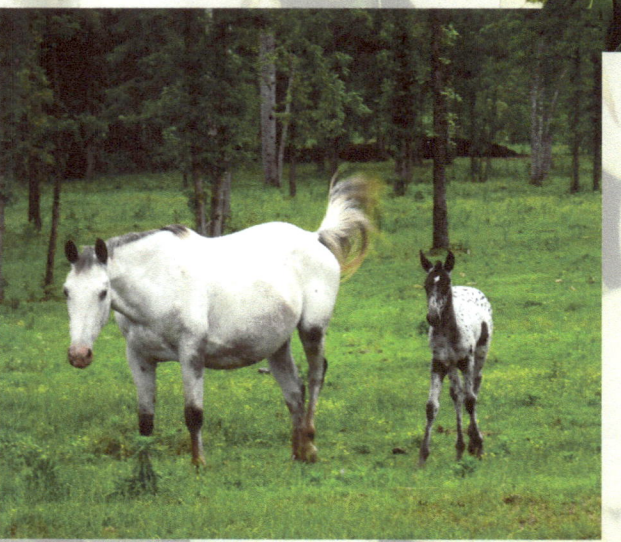

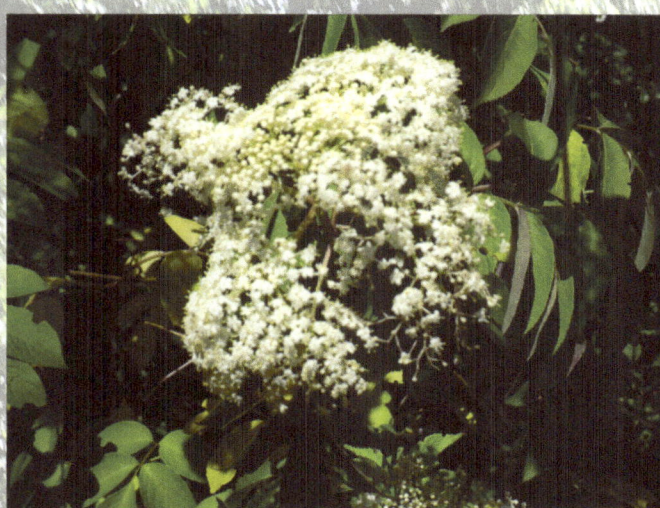

Along the way...

Spring comes to life...

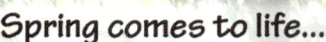

Wild flowers covering
the mountain paths fill the
heart with joy.
Elated by nature's own aromatherapy,
a breath of life engulfs your soul.

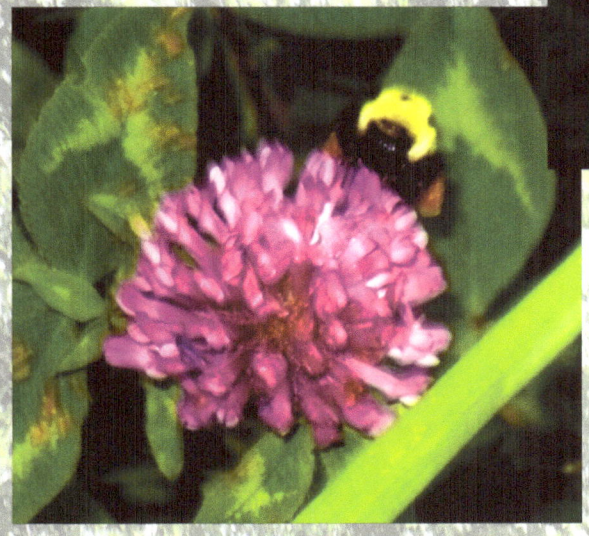

Summer

As I wonder again what life will bring,
waiting to be entertained by my muse,
the mountain opens its arms and doors,
soothing my mind while nourishing my soul.

The trees are enveloping the house,
leafy giants defusing a green glow
through the window.
The Vanilla Sky that precedes a storm is back.

Babies born to the neighbor's horses and cows
are now grazing in the pastures, playing,
no longer shadowing their moms for food.

The Jasmine has lost its blooms and scent,
the day lilies bid adieu until next year,
but the wild blackberries are ripe
and the hydrangeas are in full bloom.

Sometimes, the temperature rises to where
all life forms stand still,
waiting for dusk to pursue their musical symphony.
Fireflies are like stars shimmering in the dark,
in the hope of finding true love.

Summer, a time that spells freedom.
The relief of a school year ending and happiness
of a summer filled with excitement remain with us forever.

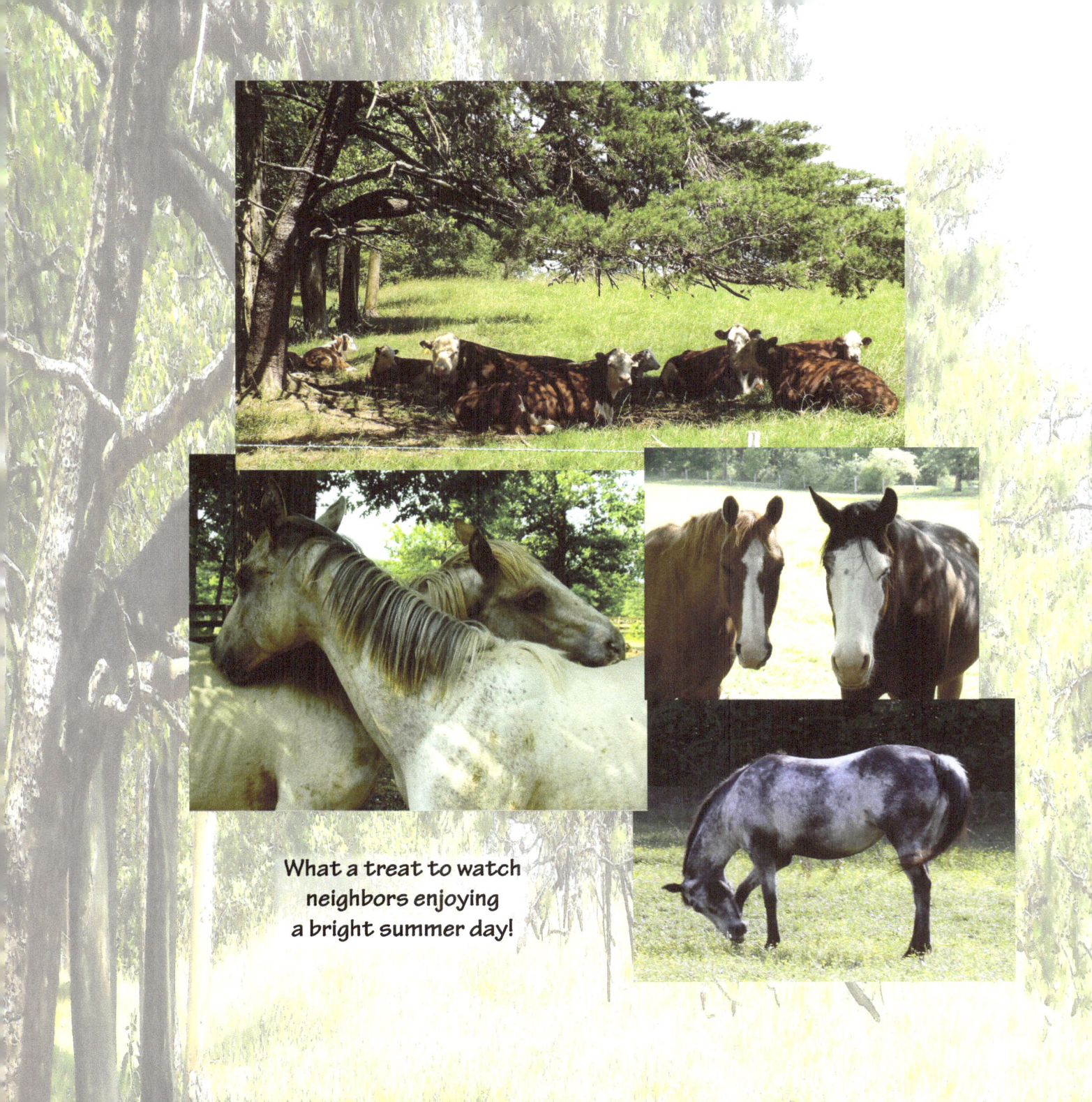

What a treat to watch
neighbors enjoying
a bright summer day!

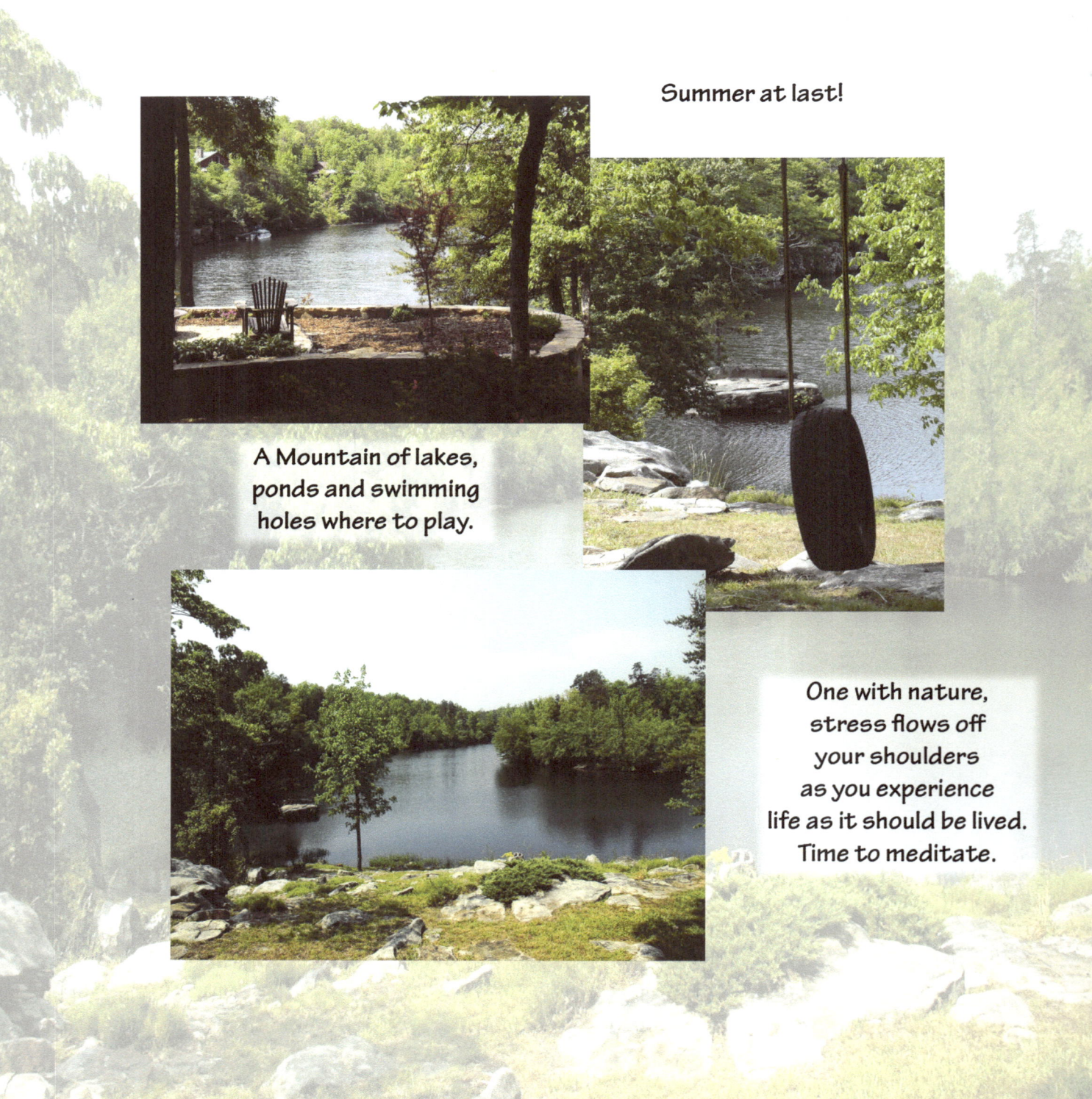

Summer at last!

A Mountain of lakes,
ponds and swimming
holes where to play.

One with nature,
stress flows off
your shoulders
as you experience
life as it should be lived.
Time to meditate.

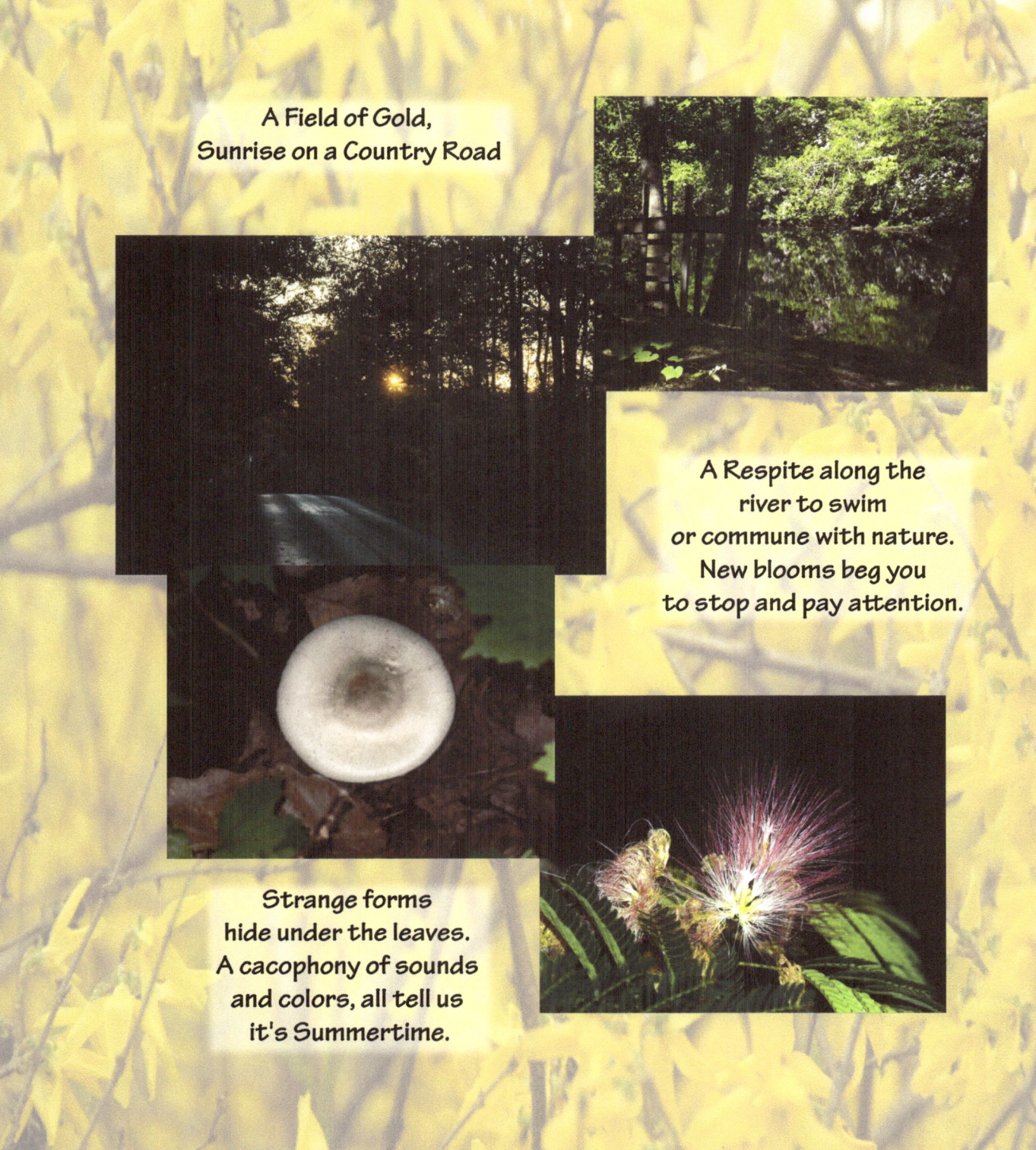

A Field of Gold,
Sunrise on a Country Road

A Respite along the
river to swim
or commune with nature.
New blooms beg you
to stop and pay attention.

Strange forms
hide under the leaves.
A cacophony of sounds
and colors, all tell us
it's Summertime.

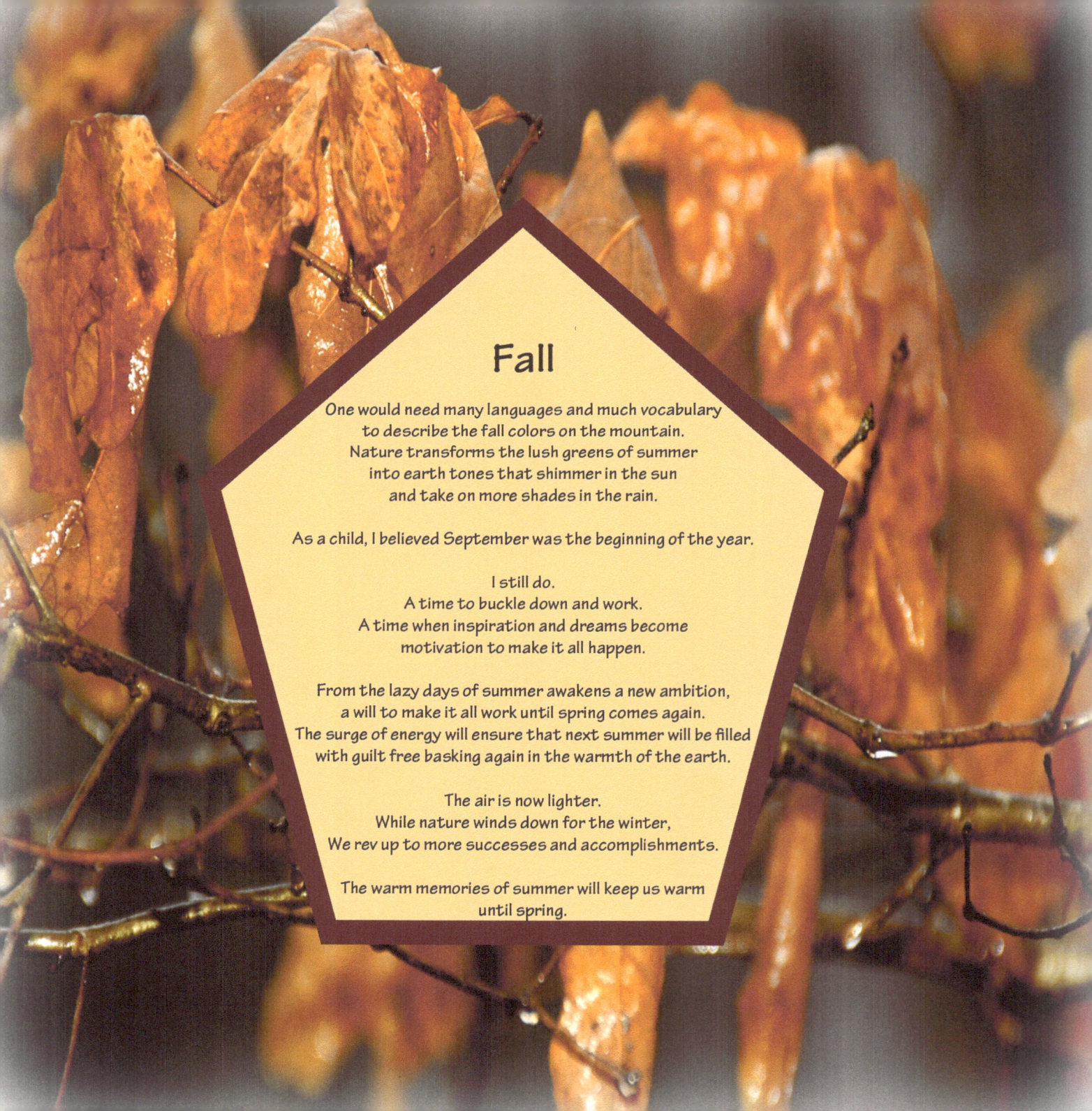

Fall

One would need many languages and much vocabulary
to describe the fall colors on the mountain.
Nature transforms the lush greens of summer
into earth tones that shimmer in the sun
and take on more shades in the rain.

As a child, I believed September was the beginning of the year.

I still do.
A time to buckle down and work.
A time when inspiration and dreams become
motivation to make it all happen.

From the lazy days of summer awakens a new ambition,
a will to make it all work until spring comes again.
The surge of energy will ensure that next summer will be filled
with guilt free basking again in the warmth of the earth.

The air is now lighter.
While nature winds down for the winter,
We rev up to more successes and accomplishments.

The warm memories of summer will keep us warm
until spring.

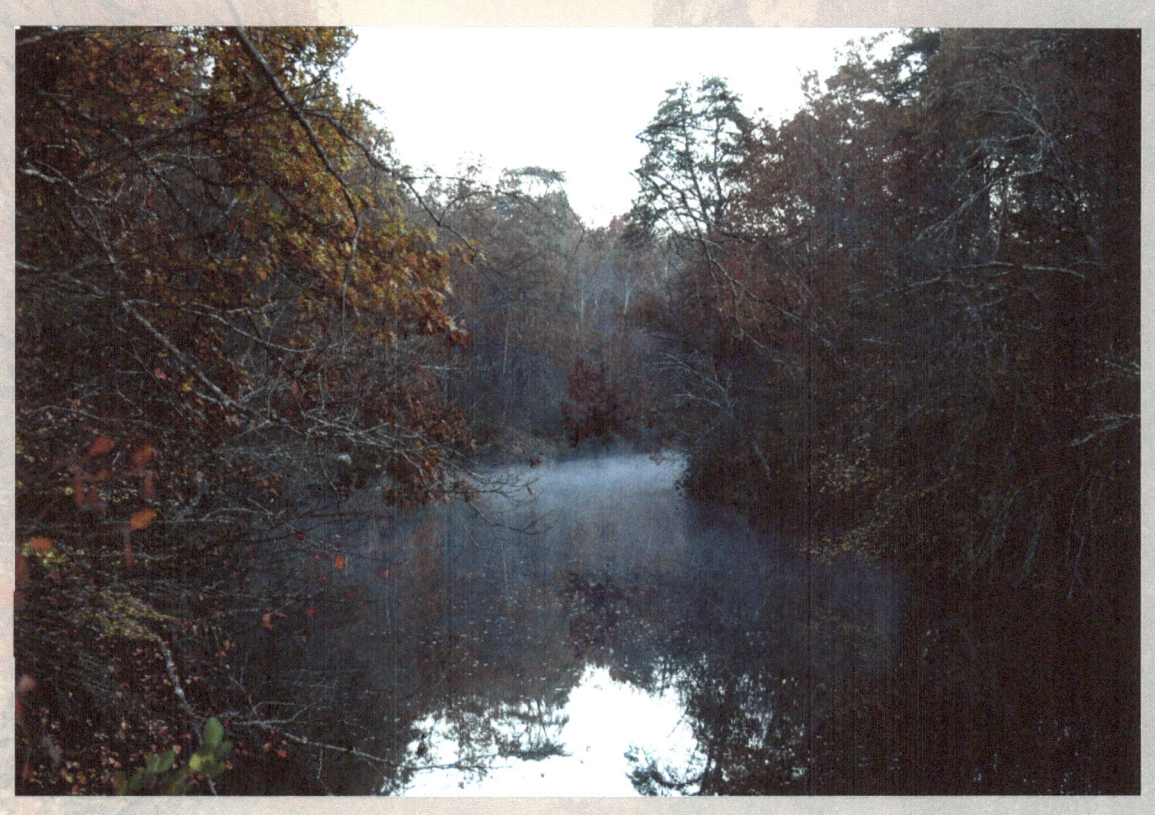

Fall is here, coloring the river
with its rich earthy tones.
Nature's paint brush is tentative
as its shades compete with
a morning mist and
the promise of a bright sunny day.

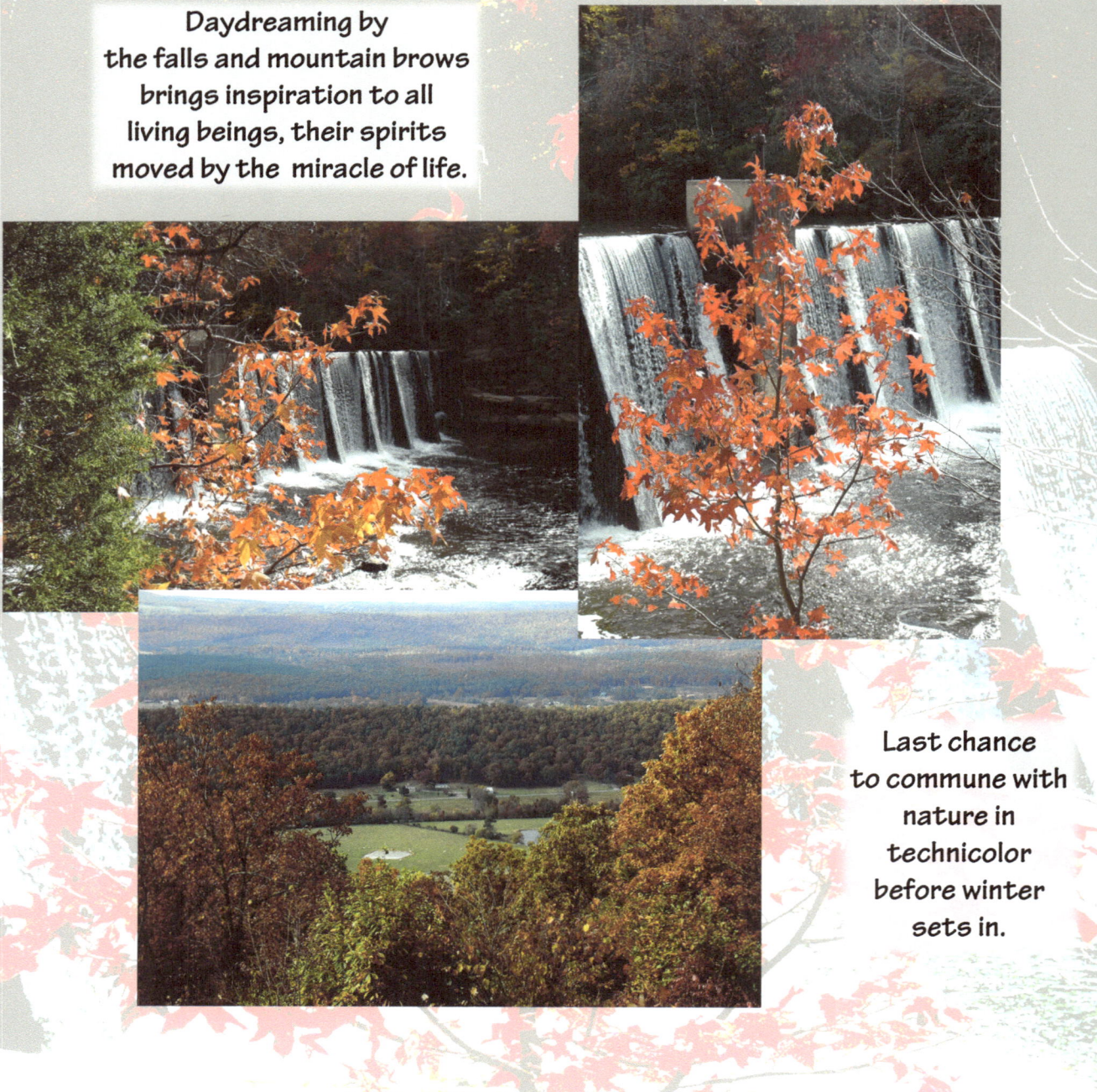

Daydreaming by
the falls and mountain brows
brings inspiration to all
living beings, their spirits
moved by the miracle of life.

Last chance
to commune with
nature in
technicolor
before winter
sets in.

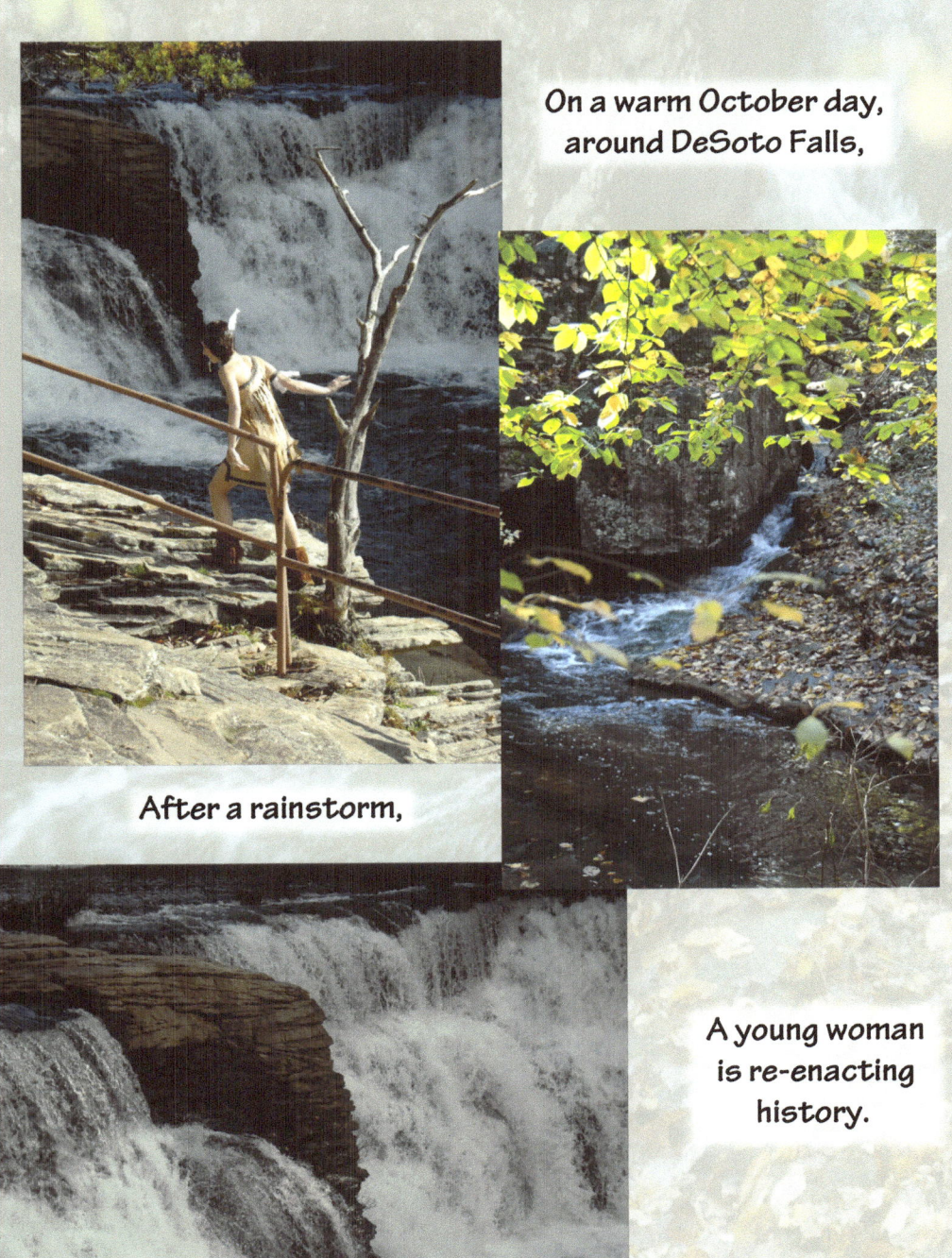

On a warm October day, around DeSoto Falls,

After a rainstorm,

A young woman is re-enacting history.

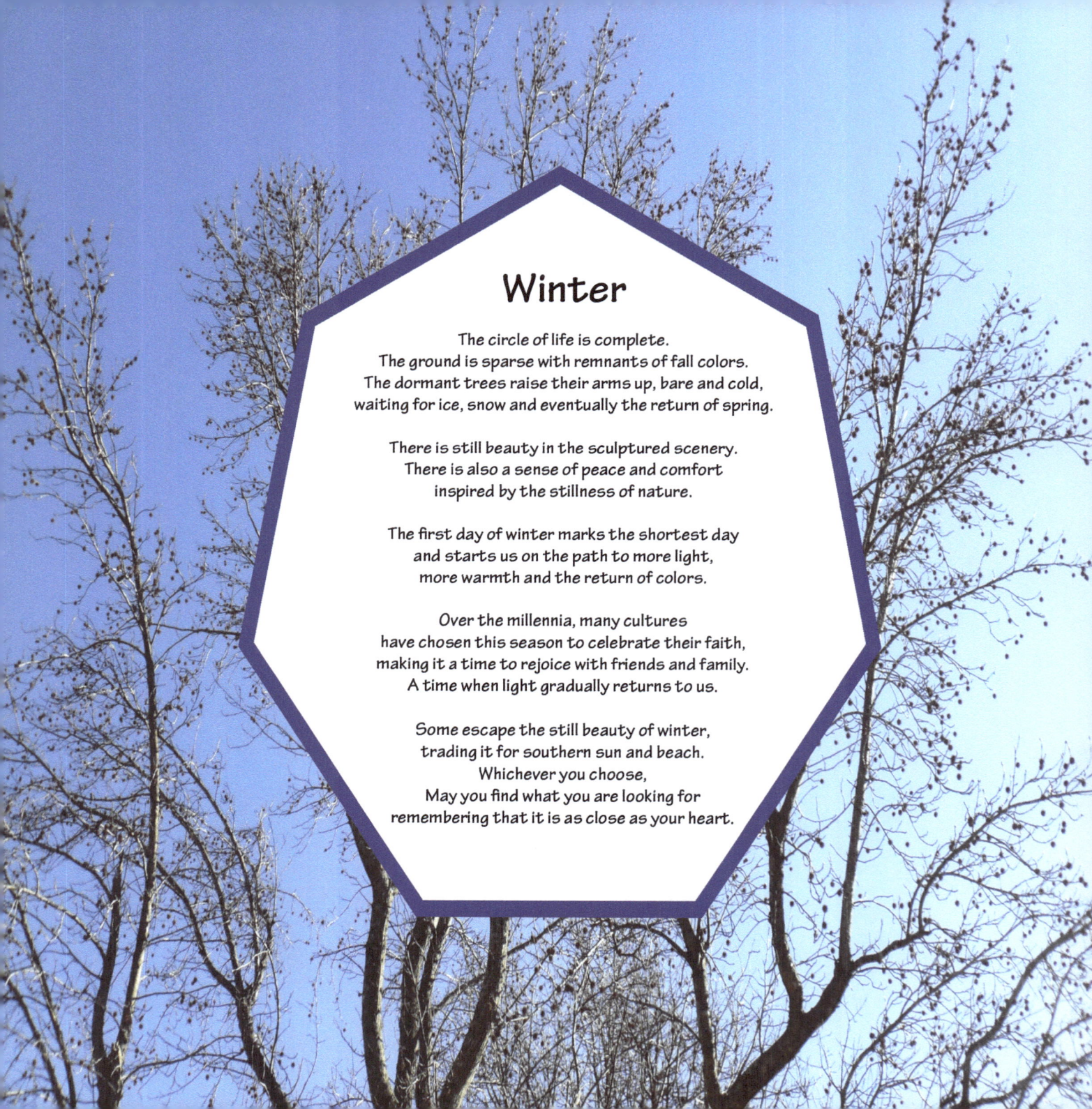

Winter

The circle of life is complete.
The ground is sparse with remnants of fall colors.
The dormant trees raise their arms up, bare and cold,
waiting for ice, snow and eventually the return of spring.

There is still beauty in the sculptured scenery.
There is also a sense of peace and comfort
inspired by the stillness of nature.

The first day of winter marks the shortest day
and starts us on the path to more light,
more warmth and the return of colors.

Over the millennia, many cultures
have chosen this season to celebrate their faith,
making it a time to rejoice with friends and family.
A time when light gradually returns to us.

Some escape the still beauty of winter,
trading it for southern sun and beach.
Whichever you choose,
May you find what you are looking for
remembering that it is as close as your heart.

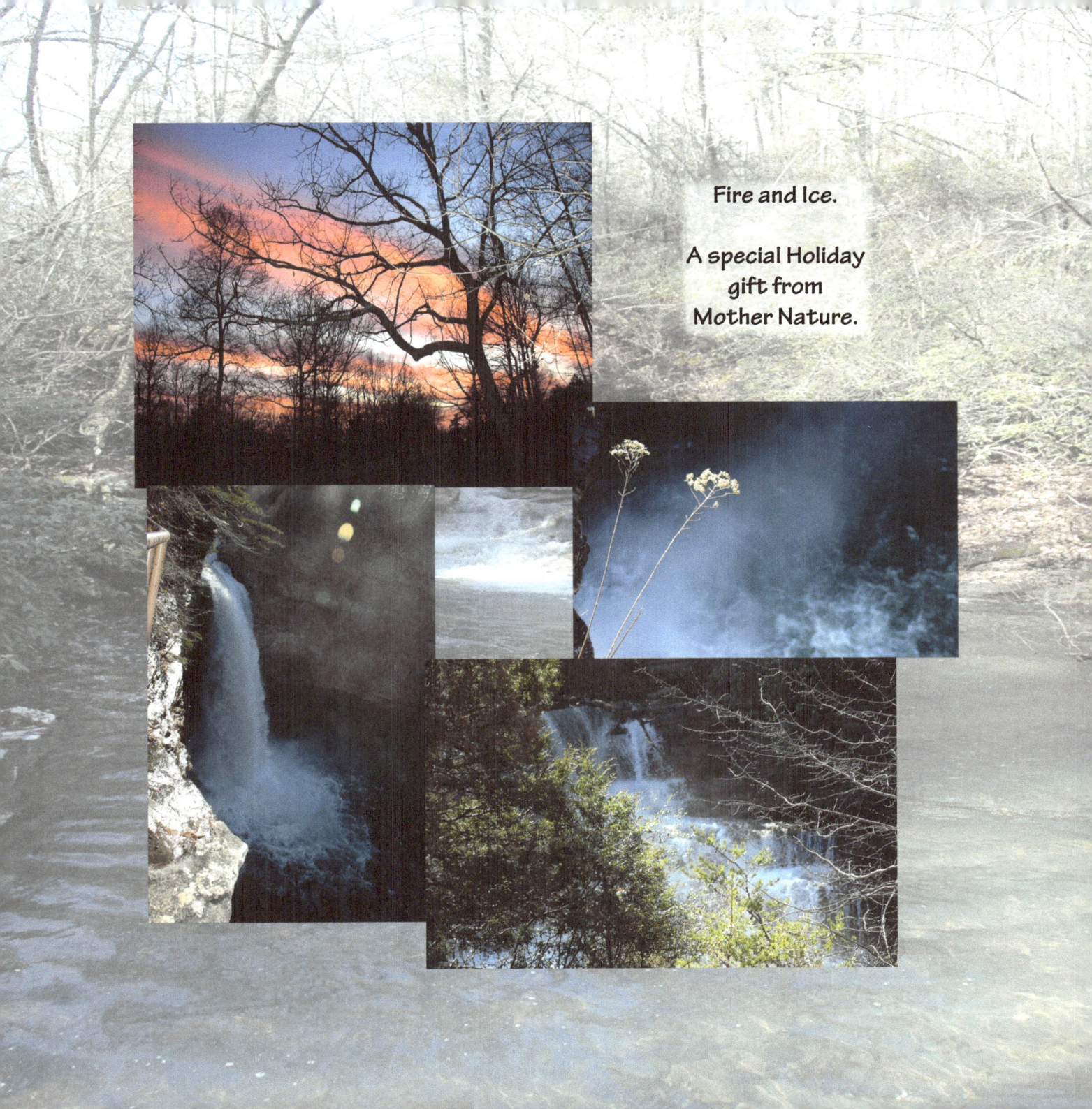

Fire and Ice.

A special Holiday
gift from
Mother Nature.

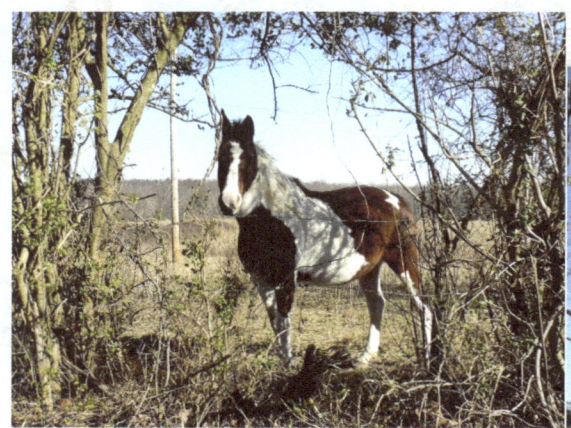

A cold, clear day,
perfect for exploring
a new trail.

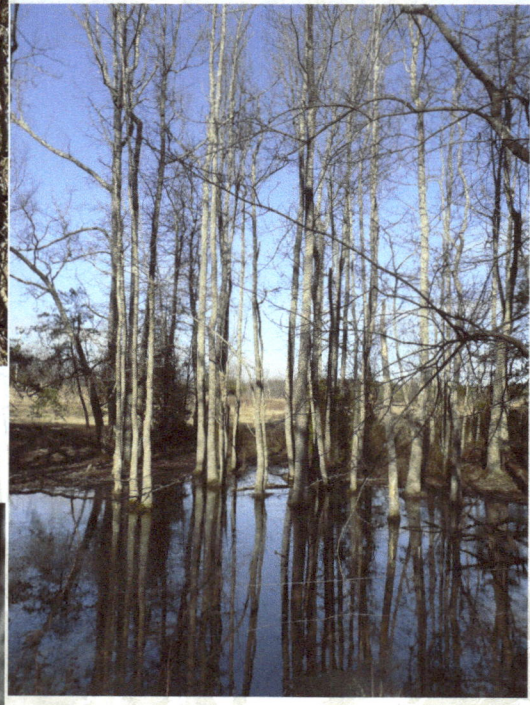

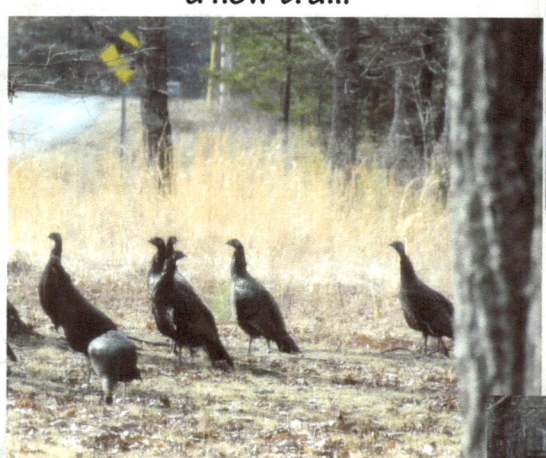

It is now safe for
wild turkeys to venture forth
as the holidays are over.

The birds can now join us
in the celebration
of a new year.

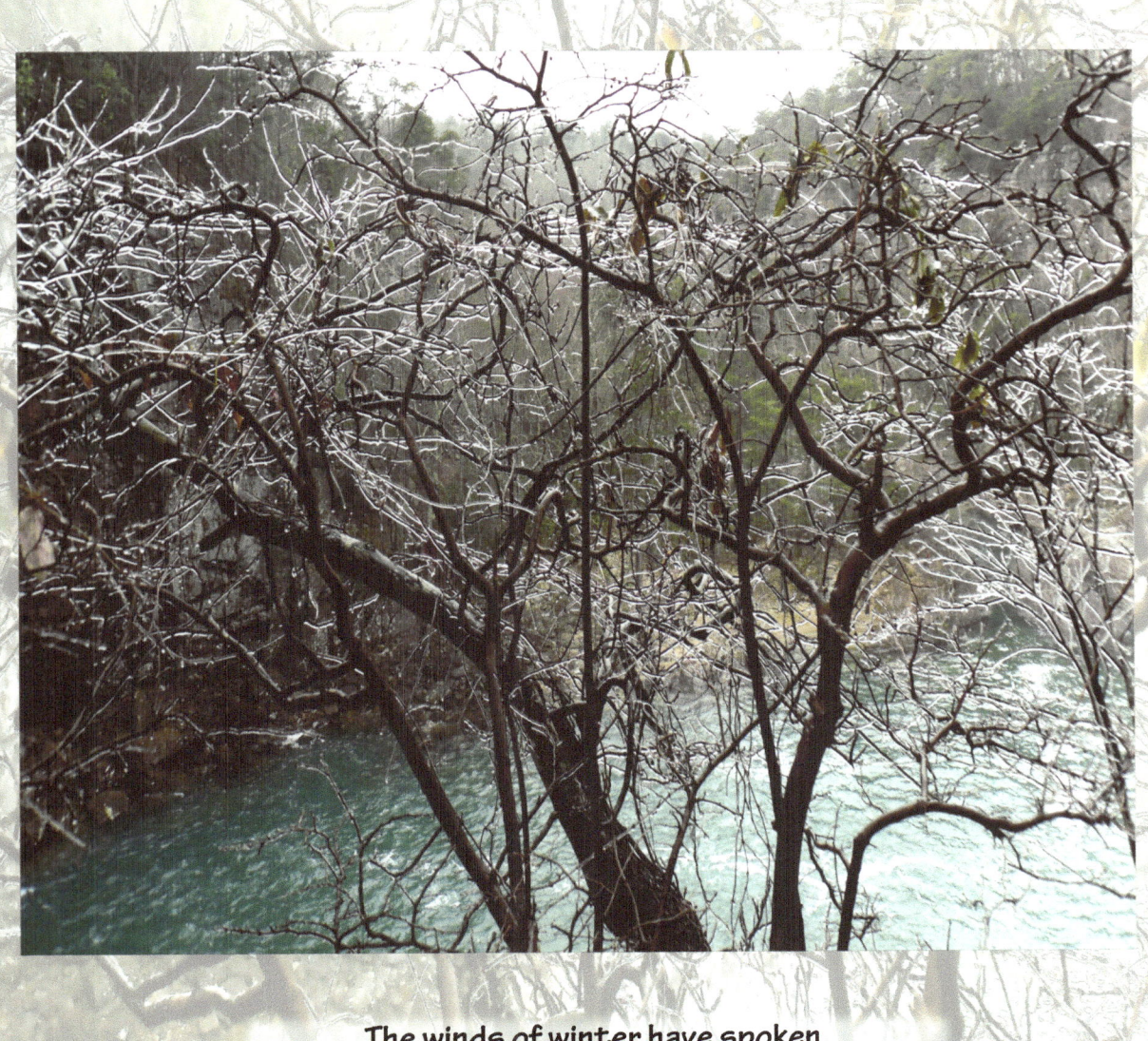

The winds of winter have spoken.
Ice crystals adorns the trees like Holiday lights,
precariously hanging from the naked branches.
Below the falls,
water stands still, as if resigned
to welcome its own glass blanket.

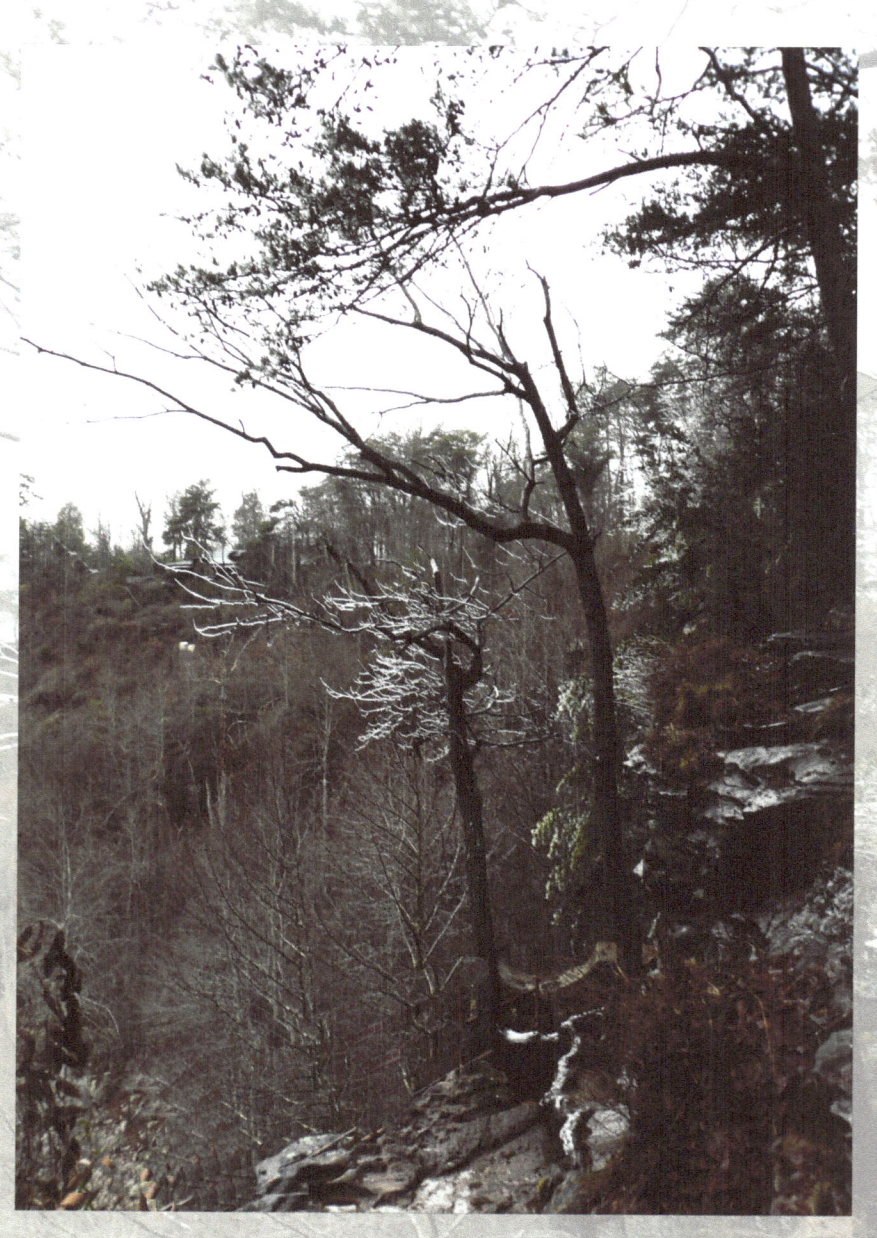

The wind is gentler,
spring is knocking at the door.
The Symphony of Life goes on...

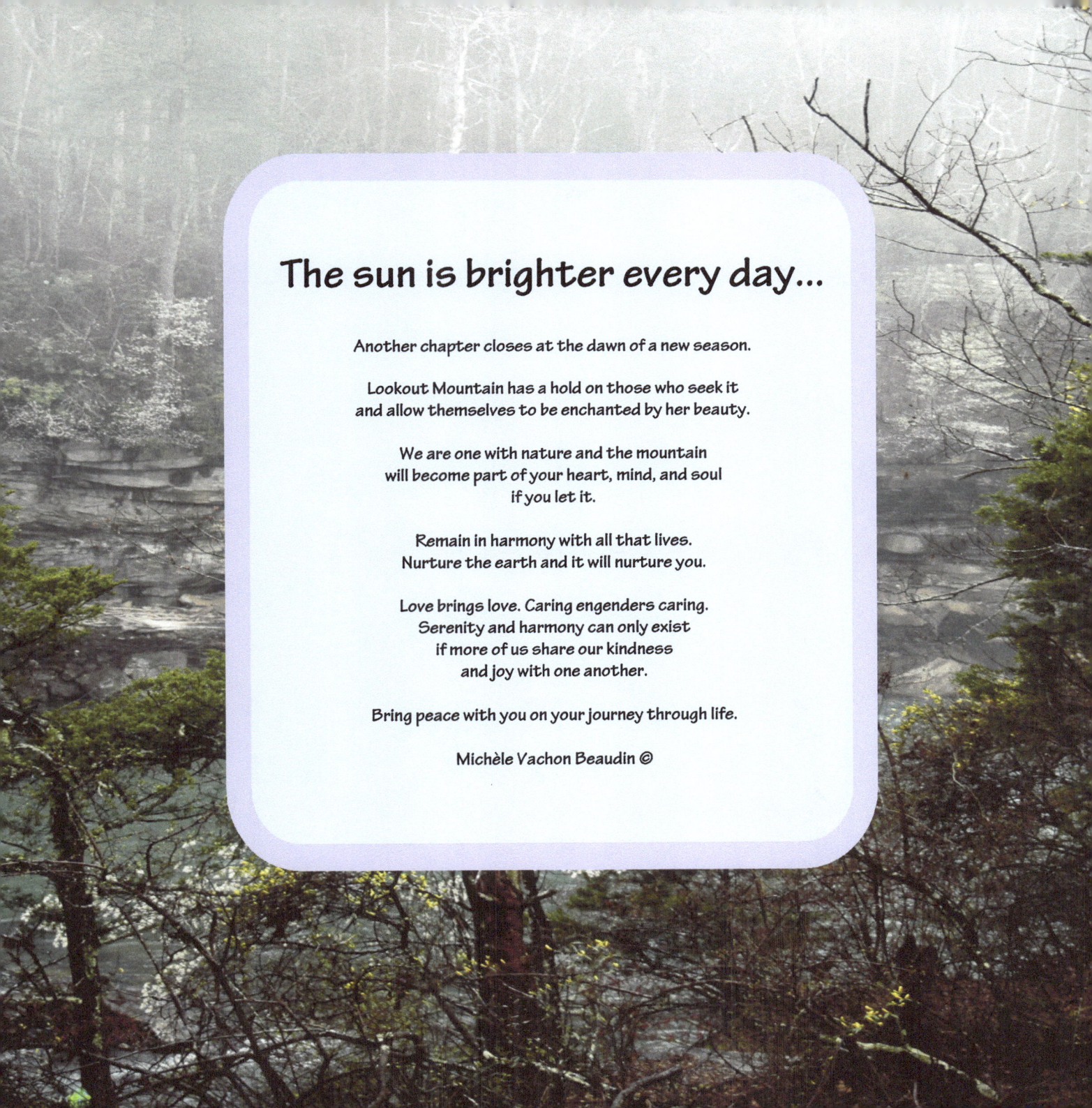

The sun is brighter every day...

Another chapter closes at the dawn of a new season.

Lookout Mountain has a hold on those who seek it
and allow themselves to be enchanted by her beauty.

We are one with nature and the mountain
will become part of your heart, mind, and soul
if you let it.

Remain in harmony with all that lives.
Nurture the earth and it will nurture you.

Love brings love. Caring engenders caring.
Serenity and harmony can only exist
if more of us share our kindness
and joy with one another.

Bring peace with you on your journey through life.

Michèle Vachon Beaudin ©

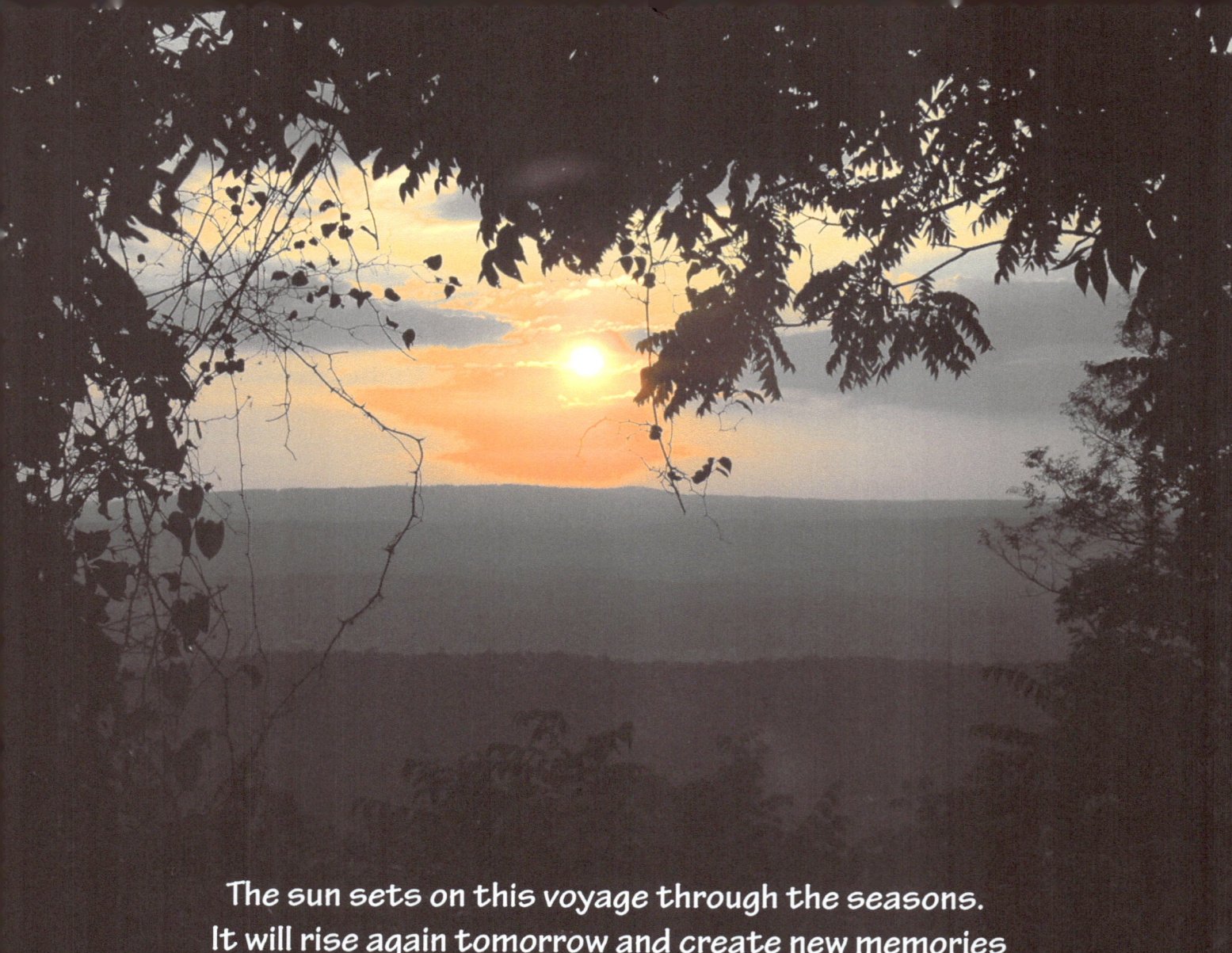

The sun sets on this voyage through the seasons.
It will rise again tomorrow and create new memories
for those who rest along its path.

Reflecting on your time communing with nature,
allow yourself to etch the memories of Lookout
Mountain with your own written words.

_____

_____

_____

_____

_____

_____

_____

_____

_____

_____

_____

_____

www.ingramcontent.com/pod-product-compliance
Lightning Source LLC
Chambersburg PA
CBHW060823290526

45792CB00005BB/1780